My Furry Foster  Family

Roo the Rabbit

by Debbi Michiko Florence
illustrated by Melanie Demmer

raintree
a Capstone company — publishers for children

For Cindy Lord, bunny-whisperer and dear friend — DMF

Raintree is an imprint of Capstone Global Library Limited, a company incorporated in England and Wales having its registered office at 264 Banbury Road, Oxford, OX2 7DY — Registered company number: 6695582

www.raintree.co.uk
myorders@raintree.co.uk

Text © Capstone Global Library Limited 2021
The moral rights of the proprietor have been asserted.

Edited by Jill Kalz
Designed by Lori Bye
Original illustrations © Capstone Global Library Limited 2021
Production by Tori Abraham
Originated by Capstone Global Library Ltd

Image credits
Capstone Studio: Karon Dubke, 66, 67 (top and bottom), 68 (right bottom), 69 (bottom); Mari Bolte: 68 (left and middle bottom), 69 (top); Melanie Demmer, 71; Roy Thomas, 70

978 1 3982 0462 1

British Library Cataloguing in Publication Data
A full catalogue record for this book is available from the British Library.

Author's note
All rescue rabbits being fostered out and adopted have a special operation so that they cannot make baby rabbits ("spaying" for females and "neutering" for males). It's important not to add to the rabbit population because there are too many rabbits that need homes already. Spaying and neutering can also help rabbits live longer lives and be calmer pets.

Printed in the United Kingdom

Contents

Dad
(Tim Takano)

Mum
(Cindy Takano)

Me
(Kaita Takano)

Eraser

Ollie

Joss Lawrence,
Happy Tails
Rescue

Hannah Miller,
my best friend

CHAPTER 1

Waiting for Roo

The day my family got our foster pet Roo was a great day. Every pet we foster is special, but Roo was *extra* special. He was our first rabbit!

My dog, Ollie, ran into my bedroom early that morning. *Yip! Yip! Yip!* He wagged his tail. I was still in bed.

"Hello, Ollie," I said with a smile.

My family and I adopted Ollie from Happy Tails Rescue. Someone had found him in a car park with no collar and no home. Now we are his forever family.

That is how we became a foster family for Happy Tails Rescue. We look after pets until they find their forever homes. We've fostered dogs, cats and even a bearded dragon!

Ollie climbed his special ramp to the top of my bed. He's a mini dachshund. His legs are short and stubby. He's not a great jumper! My dad made the ramp to help him.

Ollie licked my face and then sniffed the book in my hands.

"I'm reading about rabbits," I said. "Fostering a rabbit isn't the same as fostering a cat or dog. I've got new things to learn. I'm glad Mum brought home these books from the bookshop. I'm going to need them!"

Yip! Yip! Yip! Ollie barked and ran out of my room. He knows when someone is at our front door before the doorbell rings.

"Kaita!" Mum called. "Joss is here with the rabbit!"

Joss works for Happy Tails Rescue. She brings us foster pets. She helped us adopt Ollie.

I jumped off my bed and ran to the living room. I got there just as Mum opened the door.

"Hello, Mrs. Takano! Hey, Kaita!" Joss said. "And yes, hello, Ollie!"

Ollie wagged his tail. He even squeaked a little. He remembered Joss and how nice she was.

"Where is he?" I asked. "Where's Roo?" I tried to be polite, but I almost pushed Mum out of the way.

A carrier hung from Joss' shoulder. It looked like a big bag. Roo the rabbit was inside it. Ollie stretched his neck and tried to sniff the carrier. His tail wagged faster.

"I think Ollie should wait in your room, Kaita," Joss said. "We know he would never hurt anyone, but rabbits are prey animals."

"Do you know what *prey* means?" Mum asked me with a knowing smile.

I nodded. "Prey are animals that get hunted and eaten by predators," I said. "Like cats hunt mice or lions hunt zebras."

"Right," said Joss. "Roo will naturally be afraid of Ollie."

I picked up Ollie and put him in my room. I gave him his favourite tennis ball. "Sorry, Ollie. I'll be back for you soon," I said. I closed the door behind me.

Ollie knows the routine. He knows what it's like when my family gets a new foster pet. He actually likes chilling out in my room.

Mum and Joss were already in the spare room. Joss had set up a wire gate. She shaped it into a circle to make a pen for Roo.

"So, what is Roo's story, Joss?" Mum asked.

"Roo was an Easter gift to a child from a friend," Joss explained. "The child and her family weren't ready for a pet, though. Pets can be a lot of work. You both know that." Joss winked at Mum and me. "People need to think before adding a pet to their family."

Joss placed two bowls inside Roo's pen. She filled one with water. She put a litter tray inside the pen too.

"Is Roo litter tray-trained, like a cat?" I asked.

CHAPTER 2

Thump! THUMP!

When Joss finished setting up Roo's pen, she smiled. "OK, Kaita, are you ready to meet Roo?" she asked.

Mum laughed. "Kaita is always ready to meet a new foster pet. Aren't you, honey?" she said.

"Yep!" I said.

Joss put the carrier on the floor in the middle of the pen. She unzipped the front flap. Mum, Joss and I sat down behind the gate and waited . . . and waited . . . and waited some more.

Finally, a furry nose poked out. Then the rest of the rabbit slowly slinked out of the carrier. He was light brown and white, with floppy ears that nearly touched the floor.

"He's so cute," I said softly.

Roo looked at me. His nose twitched.

"Roo is almost five months old," Joss said. "He's a mini lop-eared rabbit and won't get much bigger. He hasn't been given much attention. Kaita, your job will be to get him used to being around people."

I leant forward and waggled my fingers at Roo. "Hello," I said.

Roo didn't run away, but he also didn't come up to me. I felt a little sad about that. I wanted to stroke him. He looked *so* soft.

"It might take time before he trusts you and other people," Joss said. "He probably won't like to be picked up. Try to teach him that people aren't scary. You can use treats to get him to trust you."

Joss and Mum stood up, and Roo turned his head towards them.

"Why don't you sit with Roo, Kaita?" Joss said. "I have a few more things to share with your mum."

"OK," I said.

Joss leaned down and put her hand on my shoulder. She spoke quietly. "Rabbits can be picky about who they choose to love," she said. "Don't be sad if he isn't very friendly with you. The most important thing you can do is teach him that he is safe here. Then, perhaps the right person will come along for him to love."

After Joss and Mum left the room, I scooted closer to Roo.

"I know we'll be great friends, Roo," I said. "Maybe not today, but it'll happen." I waggled my fingers at him again and . . .

Yip! Yip! Yip! Ollie charged into the room. Oh no! How did he get out of my bedroom?

Roo smacked the floor with his hind feet. *Thump! THUMP!*

Ollie stopped barking. He froze in his tracks.

Roo smacked the floor again. *Thump! THUMP!*

Joss and Mum hurried back to the spare room. Mum scooped up Ollie and took him out. Roo stopped thumping.

"Why was Roo stamping his feet on the floor?" I asked Joss.

"That thumping is Roo's way of saying he doesn't feel safe," Joss said.

"Oh," I said. "I'm really sorry, Roo." I started to worry. What if Joss didn't think I could do a good job with this foster pet?

Joss smiled. "I know Roo will be fine with you, Kaita," she said. "Keep this door closed, and I bet in no time you will be able to let Roo run around freely."

After Joss left, I sat down on a big bean bag, away from Roo. I grabbed my special sketchbook and started drawing.

I always draw pictures of our foster animals so I can remember them. I drew Roo drinking his water. I drew him chewing his hay. It was funny watching the long piece of hay slide bit by bit into his mouth. *Crunch! Crunch! Crunch!*

Roo didn't come over to me. And I didn't try to stroke him. It was enough to sit together in the same room, quietly. We would build our trust one day at a time.

"Good morning, Kaita," Dad said. He was making breakfast, like he does every Sunday.

"Has Mum gone on her run already?" I asked.

"Yes," Dad said. "You have time to feed Roo some treats, if you'd like." He handed me a few stems of parsley.

"Thanks!" I said, and hurried to Roo's room. Ollie didn't follow me this time. He stayed with Dad. Whenever Dad is in the kitchen, Ollie knows he will get special treats.

"Good morning, Roo," I said, opening the spare room door. "Look what I have for you."

I sat down beside Roo's pen and waved the parsley at him. He didn't come over.

I dropped a stem into the pen. Roo looked at me and twitched his nose.

After a few seconds, he hopped slowly to his treat. He kept an eye on me and sniffed. Then *chomp, chomp, chomp*! He ate it all up!

I pushed a second stem of parsley through the wires. This time Roo took it right from my hand. I held on until he had eaten most of it. When he tugged on the last short piece, I let go. He finished his snack. I was so happy he ate from my hand!

Things were going well, so I reached into Roo's pen and tried to stroke him. But he ran away. Oh, Roo! Didn't he know I wouldn't hurt him? I guess he just needed more time.

*

We followed the same routine every day during Roo's first week with us. In the morning, I fed Ollie, then Roo. I made sure Roo had plenty of hay and fresh water before I left for school. When I came home afterwards, Mum and I took Ollie on his walk. After I did my homework, I spent time with Roo.

First I cleaned Roo's pen. I stepped over the fence and scooped out his litter tray. I refreshed his hay and refilled his water bowl.

After I had finished cleaning everything, I sat down inside the pen. Roo stayed as far away from me as he could. He didn't seem scared, though. He seemed like he wanted to trust me.

The second week Roo was with us, I kept the same routine. But when I cleaned his pen, Roo did something different. He came over and sniffed my feet. I was so happy! I sat down inside his pen and held out a rabbit biscuit treat.

"Come and say hi to me, Roo," I said. "I've got a tasty bunny treat for you." I stayed very still.

Roo watched me from the other side of the pen. He blinked his brown eyes. Slowly he hopped over to me and sniffed. Then he snatched the biscuit from my hand and ran to the other side of the pen to eat it.

"Well done, Roo!" I said. "I told you we'd be great friends soon."

Two days later, I offered Roo another rabbit biscuit. He took it from me, but this time, he didn't run away to eat. This time, he stayed there in front of me. I reached out to stroke him, but he dashed away.

One evening, Dad decided it was time to let Roo stretch his legs outside the pen. First, we had to make the room safe for a rabbit.

Dad and I cleared away all the clutter from the floor. We unplugged the lamp and the computer. We made sure electrical cords were out of reach. Rabbits love to chew! Chewing electrical cords could be very dangerous for Roo.

"OK, Kaita, the room should be 'bunnyproofed' now," Dad said. "I don't think Roo will get into any trouble. Good luck! I'll be in the other room with Ollie. Shout if you need anything."

"Thanks, Dad," I said.

Dad closed the door behind him. It was just me and Roo in the room.

"Hello, Roo," I said.

Roo hopped over to me, lifted his nose and sniffed. I giggled.

By this time, he had learnt that I always had a treat. He reminded me of Ollie, when Dad is in the kitchen! Roo stood up on his hind legs and placed his front paws on the side of the pen. He stretched his body so he could get closer to me.

"You know I have a treat, don't you, Roo?" I said. "You're one clever bunny! OK, here you go."

I opened my hand and showed him his special treat: a strawberry.

Roo loved it! He grabbed the big, juicy berry, sat down and ate it up quickly. When he had finished, he looked at me and twitched his nose.

"We are going to try something new today, Roo," I said.

And do you know what? It kind of looked like my little rabbit smiled!

A few minutes later, he stepped out of the pen. He hopped under Dad's desk and sniffed. He hopped to the bookcase and sniffed the books. He hop-hop-hopped around the room, exploring. His ears flopped up and down every time he hopped. He was so cute!

Roo circled round and round the room. Then he came over to my legs. I slowly reached into my pocket and pulled out a biscuit treat. He perked his ears and waggled his nose. I put the biscuit on my leg.

Guess what? Roo hopped up and wobble-walked on my legs to get the biscuit! He ate it on my lap.

I put down another biscuit, and he ate that one too. He was really learning to trust me.

I slowly reached out my hand. *Please let me stroke you,* I thought. But, no. *Zoom!* Roo zipped back into his pen, as always. I guess he still didn't think of me as a friend.

*

Roo and I quickly got into a routine. He always took food from my hand and ate it right in front of me. But he never let me touch him.

One day, Mum said, "You know, Kaita, Roo might never let you stroke him. Some rabbits just don't like to be stroked. Remember what Joss said when she brought him here?"

"I know," I said.

"Rabbits make their own choices about people," Mum continued. "It doesn't mean he doesn't like you. He trusts you. He takes food from you. He hops up on your legs. He's even nudged your foot. Those are all good things, Kaita!"

I knew what Mum was saying was true, but I still felt sad.

Another week went by. No families were interested in adopting Roo.

I'm happy every time one of our foster pets finds a forever home. It isn't easy to let them go. Sometimes it's really hard. But that's why we foster, to find homeless pets the love they deserve. I wanted that for Roo.

In the meantime, I gathered lots of toys for him to play with. He nudged a ball across the room. He threw a toilet roll tube in the air. His favourite toy was a cat tunnel. He zoomed through it and made it crinkle. I always laughed when he did that. Rabbits are fast!

Then the day came that I had been hoping for . . . sort of. Dad, Mum and I were eating dinner. Ollie was curled up beneath my chair.

"Guess what?" Dad said, through a mouthful of pizza.

I had a feeling I knew what he was going to say. It felt like my heart sank into my stomach along with the pizza I'd eaten.

"Joss called today," Dad continued. "A family might want to adopt Roo."

"When?" I asked.

"They're coming over tomorrow," Mum said. "Joss is coming too."

That was strange. Usually, Joss talks to people who want to adopt an animal first. If they're a good fit, she'll send them to our house to meet the pet. If all goes well, the people take the pet home.

"Why is Joss coming?" I asked.

"This family already has a rabbit," Dad said. "They used to have two rabbits that had bonded, like best friends. The older rabbit died. Now the family is looking for a new friend for the younger bunny."

"Sometimes rabbits don't get on with each other," Mum added. "Joss is going to show us how to do a 'meet and greet' with the family's rabbit. She'll make sure everything goes well."

I taught Roo a lot of things, but I didn't teach him to like other rabbits. I worried about how Roo would behave.

CHAPTER 5

Love at first sight

Joss came to our house first the next day. I was in the spare room with Roo, sitting on the floor. Well, *I* was sitting and *he* was running all over the place! When Joss walked in, though, he stopped. He hopped over to me and lay on his belly. He stretched his back legs out behind him.

"It shows a lot of trust that he lies down next to you," Joss said with a wink. "You've done a great job with him, Kaita."

"I wish he would let me stroke him," I said. "Every time I try, he runs away."

"I know," Joss said. "But for him to trust you is wonderful. The hope is that he bonds with the other family and their rabbit. You've done everything to make sure he's ready for that."

Joss and I moved Roo and his things into my bedroom. She said rabbits can get upset when other animals come into their space. Roo's space was the spare room. Hopefully, meeting in my room would make both rabbits feel more safe.

Yip! Yip! Yip! Ollie ran full speed to the front door.

The doorbell rang.

"Here we go," Joss said. She and I walked to the living room. Mum was holding Ollie. A smiling family stood in the doorway.

"Kaita, this is Mr and Mrs Castaldo and their daughters, Nora and Willow," Joss said.

Nora looked like the big sister. Willow looked closer to my age. I wondered what it would be like to have a sister.

"This is our rabbit, Felicia," Willow said. She pointed to the carrier her dad was holding.

"Let's take her to Kaita's room," Joss said. "Roo's waiting for us in there."

Mum and Mrs Castaldo stayed in the living room with Ollie. My room is not very big. It felt even smaller with Joss, Mr Castaldo, Willow, Nora, Roo, Roo's pen and me crammed inside it!

Mr Castaldo put the carrier down near the pen. Nora opened it, and out came Felicia.

"She's so pretty," I said.

Unlike Roo's ears, Felicia's went straight up. She looked like she was wearing a black mask and hat, a white shirt and black trousers.

"Come here, Felicia," Willow said. She tapped the floor in front of her.

Felicia hopped straight up to Willow, and Willow stroked her!

I gasped. "Will she let *me* stroke her?" I asked.

"Yes," Nora said. "Felicia loves people."

I tapped the floor like Willow had. I held my breath, and Felicia hopped over to me. I reached out my hand, expecting her to run away, like Roo always did. But Felicia didn't run away. I gently stroked her head. She was so soft!

"Well, look at Roo," Joss said. "He wants to see what all the fuss is about."

Roo had hopped to the edge of his pen to be closer to us. He was watching Felicia. His ears and nose twitched.

Felicia spotted Roo and slowly hopped over to him. Roo was still in his pen, just in case they didn't get on. We didn't want the rabbits to fight and get hurt.

Felicia and Roo sniffed each other through the wires. Then Roo hopped over to his hay and started to eat.

"This is very good," Joss said. "They're behaving like they're not bothered by each other at all. Kaita, why don't you let Roo out? Let's see what happens."

I opened the gate and held out a strawberry. But before I could call Roo, Felicia hopped right up to me and snatched it from my hand!

We all laughed. "I guess Felicia likes strawberries too!" I said.

Roo saw that Felicia had eaten his treat. He hopped over and sniffed my empty hand.

Luckily for Roo, I had two more strawberries. I held one in each hand. Roo ate one, and Felicia ate the other. Sweet!

After their treats, Felicia took a few steps towards Roo. She put her head down on the ground right in front of him. We all waited. Joss stood ready to separate them, just in case they started to fight.

"Felicia wants Roo to lick her fur," Joss whispered. "It will show her that he wants to be friends. If he does, that means love at first sight."

I held my breath. This was a big moment for our little rabbit.

Roo waggled his nose and started licking Felicia's head.

"Hooray! They're a match!" Nora said.

The meet and greet couldn't have gone better. Roo found his forever family! I was so happy for him. He finally had people to love him and take care of him. He had a new bunny friend too.

"Kaita, do you want to say goodbye to Roo before he leaves?" Joss asked. She knew how hard it was going to be to watch Roo go.

I nodded and put a biscuit on my leg. Roo hopped over, climbed up and ate his treat on my lap. Did he know this was goodbye? He had been in our house for almost a month. He felt like a part of our family.

"Goodbye, Roo," I said. "I hope you have a long, happy life."

I reached out a finger to try to stroke him one last time. I expected him to run away. Except he didn't. He stayed still as I stroked his nose with my finger. Just once. Then he leapt off my lap. It was like he said goodbye to me. Now I didn't feel so sad.

Joss said that rabbits choose who they love. I was glad Roo chose Felicia. And I was glad he let me say goodbye.

Think about it!

1. What are some things that Kaita does to try to gain Roo's trust?
2. List a few big and small differences between Roo and Felicia.
3. What are some important things to remember when caring for a rabbit?

Draw it! Write it!

1. Draw a picture of Roo.
2. Roo thumps his hind feet on the floor when he is afraid or angry. Think about a time when *you* were afraid or angry. What did you say and do? Write a letter to Kaita about it.

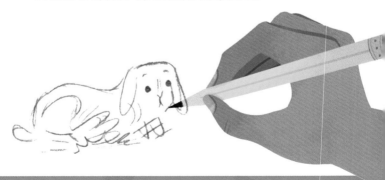

Glossary

adopt   take and raise as one's own

bond   have a close relationship

carrier   box or bag that carries or holds something

dachshund   type of dog with a long body and short legs

foster   give care and a safe home for a short time

litter tray   container indoors in which a pet goes to the toilet

parsley   plant with small flat or crinkly leaves, often used to decorate food

predator   animal that hunts other animals for food

prey   animal hunted by another animal for food

routine   set of tasks done in a set order

trust   depend on others, to believe that they will be honest and fair

Furry feelings

Kaita Takano is a made-up character, but she is based on a real-life Kaita, who also fosters pets with her family. Real Kaita says that rabbits use body language to show how they feel. People do too, in addition to speaking.

Let's compare the ways rabbits and Real-Life Kaita express themselves. Then compare them to what *you* do or say!

THRILLED

A rabbit runs and leaps in the air.

Kaita says, "This was the best day ever!"

RELAXED

A rabbit lies on her belly, with her back legs stretched out.

Kaita does some crafting, drinks tea or knits.

NEEDS ATTENTION

A rabbit nudges your foot and hand or rubs her chin on you.

Kaita talks about something funny from her day.

HAPPY

A rabbit quietly
grinds her teeth, like
when a cat purrs.

Kaita decorates cupcakes,
plays with her pony (Angus)
and cuddles her pets!

SCARED/ANGRY

A rabbit thumps her hind feet loudly on the ground.

Kaita knits - furiously!

ANNOYED

A rabbit turns her back on you. If she's really annoyed, she will hop away and kick her feet back at you.

Kaita says, **"Whaaaat?!"**

About the author

Debbi Michiko Florence writes books for children in her writing studio, The Word Nest. She is an animal lover with a degree in zoology and has worked at a pet shop, the Humane Society, a raptor rehabilitation centre and a zoo. She is the author of two chapter book series: Jasmine Toguchi and Dorothy & Toto. Debbi lives in Connecticut, USA, with her husband, a rescue dog, a rabbit and two ducks.

About the illustrator

Melanie Demmer is an illustrator and designer living in Los Angeles, USA. She graduated with a BFA in illustration from the College for Creative Studies in Detroit and has been creating artwork for various clothing, animation and publishing projects ever since. When she isn't making art, Melanie enjoys writing, spending time in the great outdoors, iced tea, scary films and having naps with her cat, Pepper.

Go on all the fun, furry foster adventures!

Apple and Annie, the Hamster Duo

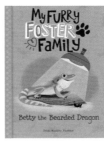

Betty the Bearded Dragon

Buttons the Kitten

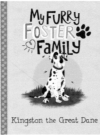

Kingston the Great Dane

Murray the Ferret

Roo the Rabbit

Tiki the Cockatoo

Toby the Dog

Only from Raintree!